To Olive + Mike

C000300536

TRUFFLES' DIARY:
ONE YEAR ON

You've read the first book —
hope this one comes up
to "scratch".

Luv Truffles x

Shiela

TRUFFLES' DIARY:
ONE YEAR ON

More Mewsings from the Fat Tabby Cat

As told by Truffles
with a little help from
Sheila Collins

APEX PUBLISHING LTD

First published in 2006 by
Apex Publishing Ltd
PO Box 7086, Clacton on Sea, Essex, CO15 5WN, England

www.apexpublishing.co.uk

British Library Cataloguing-in-Publication Data
A catalogue record for this book
is available from the British Library

ISBN 1-904444-68-7

Typeset in 12.5pt Lucida Sans

Production Manager: Chris Cowlin

Cover Design: Andrew Macey

Printed and bound in Great Britain

FOREWORD

Anyone who has owned an ageing, fat, spoiled cat will immediately recognise the one in this book. Truffles is confident in her human slaves, snoozing on the sun warmed patio of her Cornish home and reminiscing about past events.

Those of who you have read that first collection of these feline memoirs - Truffles' Diary - will recognise some of the cast of four legged creatures but there are some new additions in the shape of a pair of kittens next door.

My own cats, Pugwash the Second and Arbuthnot would just love this book. What a pity they can't read - or then again perhaps not. They might learn too much about controlling humans!

- **Ann Widdecombe**

GETTING TO KNOW ME!

Hello people - well this is Truffles again, one year on from when I let you first see my diary! I was most gratified that so many of you bought it and enjoyed it! For those of you who never read it, shame on you! Go out and get it! My fans from the first book may want to skip the intro - but for those who never read it, here is a brief note of my background, and this time I shall be telling you more about my pals from the past!

I am now seventeen years old, which is eighty-something in your human years, but I only admit to old age very slowly creeping on, as my fur is as thick and glossy as ever and I have no aches and pains yet and can still put on a turn of speed when I want to. However, as I have my personal carers to attend to my every whim, most of my time now is spent just lazing around, sleeping and reminiscing over events from the past. In this second little book, I am going to recall more amusing things that have happened over the years. The older you get the further back your memory seems to go, so I can remember even more things now than I could last year!

First of all, I must give you the cast list! The most important first - me! The others follow!

My friend Tansy and I were picked from a cats' refuge when we were only six weeks old by our human carers, Sheila and Peter. Both Tansy and I had been abandoned with our other siblings, but I do not want to dwell on our short lives before that. Suffice to say that the good life really began when we were taken back to Peter and Sheila's place in Cornwall where we joined a household of various other cats, a St Bernard dog, a macaw and tropical fish indoors and pond fish outdoors. Something for all tastes really - fur, feather and fin.

I am a tabby with an immaculate, evenly striped coat of co-ordinating tans and browns, while Tansy wore a black-and-white long-furred catsuit. The other cats were Lucky, who was pale ginger and white; Taro, an aristocat, who called himself a Birman and who had a super couture coat of pale cream with a seal trim; and finally Robbie, who was a bright shade of ginger and white. Sadly Robbie only had one eye due to a tumour, but this never seemed to bother him and actually didn't make him look odd - he just looked as if he was winking at you!

The place in Cornwall was terrific for all of we pets: a large garden of about ¾ acre that had lots of vegetation and hiding places - a shrubbery, flower beds and rockeries - bordered on one side by a large natural pond of about 60 metres in length and 10 metres across with an island in the middle, and on two other sides by open fields with horses in one and occasionally young cows in the other. We felt as if we were living in a park, and Robbie, in particular, who had spent most of his earlier life, being adopted, living in a small town flat, was always amazed at the open expanse of grass. He thought he was in paradise. When he first joined the gang he was quite frightened of this large expanse of bright green. Up until then all he could remember was being indoors with an elderly human all the time and the only view he got of the great outdoors was looking through a window at a narrow street.

Readers of my diary will know that Lucky, who was ever my preferred companion over all the others, was a fount of knowledge and spent hours telling me about things that had happened both to himself and to other previous pets in the family. So in this little book I freely admit that most of the anecdotes I mention that had occurred before I arrived on the scene were told to me by Lucky. For example, he said that Sheila and Peter some time earlier had two other cats called Sasha and Coco. They were half-sisters but couldn't have looked more unalike. Sasha was a very long-furred, pure white glamour puss with one blue eye and one green eye. Coco was a dark brown tortoiseshell colour, also long furred. They originated from Liverpool (as did posh Taro coincidentally) and Lucky used to say that his broad Cornish accent and their Liverpool ones, together with Taro's rather affected hoity-toity tones, made up a really interesting cats' chorus! Sasha and Coco moved to the big house and garden together with Taro and Lucky initially, but sadly both of them had passed on to that big cat basket in the sky just before Tansy and I were taken in.

The St Bernard dog was called Hennessy, and Lucky told me that he came into the humans' household as a six-week-old pup to join their basset hound, Lady, who was getting on a bit in years. Lady, the humans thought, would be a good influence on Hennessy and help to train him. Well, said Lucky, that was a laugh! She was as dim as a Toc H lamp and he wasn't much better! However, she perked up when Hennessy was around and Sheila always said it probably extended her life. Lady sadly didn't make it for the family's move to the country house - pity, because she would have been in seventh heaven wandering around the huge grounds sniffing here, there and everywhere.

The feathered member of the group was Geronimo, the blue and gold macaw. He was a real pain to we cats - always shouting and screeching and saying things that really well-bred felines wouldn't dream of uttering. However, we did remember certain words he shouted at us and stored them up in case we ever needed to use them in a real cats' shouting match!

Now, of course, the human carers and I have moved away from our previous home and are ensconced in a different part of Cornwall - still very pleasant, but with a much smaller garden. My needs are fully met, however, as we have a delightful patio area and that is all I really want nowadays - something warm to snooze on. Some good weather would help - it's been a bit lacking this spring so far, but hopefully we look forward to a good summer dose of those lovely warm rays of sunshine.

My neighbour, Pandy, the wimp with the limp, is still around, of course, but now they have two new additions to their family: two lovely young kittens called Milly and Lily arrived just after Christmas.

Well, that is the cast now introduced, so over this coming week, as I once more record my daily activities for your interest and, I hope, amusement, I shall get the memory into gear and try to recall more funny things from the past to tell you.

Sunday:
8.30am   Well things haven't changed for the better over this past year as far as my too early wake-up call is concerned. Peter came noisily into the kitchen, disturbing me as usual, and then proceeded to hustle me out of my comfy bed and show me the open door into the garden. Well, he showed it to me - and I looked at it - but in no way was I going out! It was far too early and also that nasty wet dew all over the grass did not encourage me in the least. So I sat firmly on my backside just

inside the door and waited whilst he brushed the carpet around my toilet area and changed yesterday's cat litter. In my diary last year I let slip the fact that I rather enjoyed the pastime of scattering litter around as far as I could so that I could also enjoy watching him bending up and down and brushing it all up again. Unfortunately, Peter read this and it motivated him into buying me a new enclosed litter box. This monstrosity is rather like an igloo and with just the small entrance at the front it is now far more difficult for me to scoop bits of litter out. However, I do my best and I'm pleased to say there is always something outside of it for him to sweep up.

8.45am   The bits of litter duly tidied and the fresh granules loaded into the igloo, Peter now morphed into my coiffeuse and, with comb and brushes to the fore, he lifted me onto the table and gave me my weekly fur-do. I quite like this procedure; well, the brushing part - not so sure about the comb, particularly when he is combing out the odd tangle in my tail or trousers. I saw a large heap of old fur gradually mounting on the tabletop. I seem to be moulting a lot this year - perhaps this is a sign of a good, hot summer approaching. Anyway, five minutes or so later, I emerged a new cat with my catsuit shining nicely in the rays of the morning sun that were now pouring through the kitchen window and back door (the latter still open in Peter's vain attempt to get me outside!)

9.00am   At last the best bit of the morning procedure, breakfast. Today it was a pâté of salmon and herbs - quite refreshing on an early summer's day and I soon finished it off. Peter had disappeared into the part of the house where his motor machines live, so I was left alone in the kitchen to wash my face and whiskers and do my general ablutions. Sheila had still not appeared - she loves her bed as much as I love mine!

9.10am   I decided I would, in fact, put my nose out of the back door since Peter was not there to harass me or to see that I had succumbed to his wish of getting me outside in the first place. A cat should never, but never, make the human carers think he/she is under their power. Cats do things THEY wish to do, not what other people want them to do. If the cat's wishes and the human's coincide, well all that does is to make the humans think they DO have the power, but of course we all know that they do not! Over hapless dogs maybe, but certainly not we cats!

9.15am   I sat on the back-door mat and enjoyed the sun for a while. Then all of a sudden I noticed Pandy, my admirer from next door, limping towards me. As readers of my previous book will know, he worships the ground I walk on and if I walked on water he would probably drown trying to follow me there too! Such a pity he is not a better figure of a cat - he has this disability with his walking, probably caused by a car accident when he was young or he may even have been like it since birth. Nobody seems to know. I do not mean to be unkind - he is actually quite good looking and wears his immaculate black-and-white catsuit rather well and with a certain style. People often compare him to a certain cartoon cat who advertises cat food. Despite the fact that he is something of a loner and quite often spends the nights outdoors curled up on the earth under bushes or cuddled into a nice comfy compost heap, his white bits always look squeaky clean and his claws are neat and short. I always notice these things, being very fussy about cleanliness myself. Unlike dogs, generally cats keep themselves extremely clean of their own volition, and for cats living in human environments as pets, this also avoids the necessity of their being given the horrid wet baths that dogs have to endure.

9.30am   Pandy lay down on the patio a few paving stones away from me with his head on his paws, surveying me. Perversely, even though I am not really attracted to him myself, I felt glad that my coat was newly groomed and that I looked at my best in the sunlight. My variegated brown and golden stripes shone in rather a delightful manner and he was obviously transfixed and probably envious. Even though I am many years older than him, we ladies of a certain age have a particular pride in being able to attract a toy boy. However, it has only really been Lucky, a real swashbuckling hero of my cat world, who has ever attracted me. Lucky was part of our group at the previous house, and in this year's diary most of the stories I intend to tell you were told to me by him when we were snuggled up together during the winter evenings. Though we were close, we were not that close since we were both missing certain parts, which was the one power that Sheila and Peter did have over us! They did not wish for any more cats than their chosen few, and I suppose I can understand this - after all, there will never be another Truffles!

11.00am Well, I was still lying on the patio and I must have been in quite a deep sleep because I never heard Sheila emerge out of the kitchen and it was only when she nearly stepped on me whilst bringing out the washing to hang out that I saw her. Talking of washing - this is yet another human example of wasting time and energy. Why on earth do they need so many different outer coverings? No wonder they get fed up with all the washing and ironing of these unnecessary items - Sheila is always moaning on about how she loathes ironing. Cats never have to do ironing! With just one catsuit, all you need is to give yourself an all over wash each day and your fur comes up sparkling and there is just no need for all this excess. Will humans never understand? They just use up so much energy on these thankless tasks - cats are infinitely more sensible regarding these things.

1.30pm   Lunchtime and I wandered back in and found a snack waiting for me in my bowl. Sheila and Peter had gone out to meet some other humans for their own lunch. Sheila always tries to get out of cooking their Sunday roast by suggesting that the one provided in that local place, where humans like to drink those awful sickly drinks, is much better than the one she can prepare.

1.40pm   Lunch finished, I strolled into the dining room and settled down on my rug in front of the patio doors, which is my favourite place to sleep, daydream and remember. Pandy positioned himself outside and we both slept.

4.30pm   I awoke, had a nice stretch and prepared to recall some moments from the past. You remember that I told you that Sheila and Peter have had several cats. Well, their first pets were two half-sisters called Sasha and Coco. I heard all about them from Lucky, but they had departed for the big runway and taken off to the giant cat basket in the sky before I came on the scene. Lucky told me that Sheila had worked in an office and they had a head office in Liverpool (some other place that I don't believe is in Cornwall) and she got friendly with another human who worked there and kept lots of cats. Sasha arrived first and Coco the following season. Sasha was snowy-white with a very large and fluffy tail (useful in the summer for keeping the midges away!), but Coco was a tortoiseshell colour with - unlike my nice, even, symmetrical stripes - odd patches of colours ranging from pale gold to dark brown. Sounds rather a mishmash to me, but Lucky said she looked quite unusual and everyone seemed to remark on her. Unlike Sasha, who was very elegant and behaved in a ladylike manner, Coco was rather a tomboy. She often got into trouble and Lucky remembered that one day, whilst the humans were out, Coco was investigating a wash boiler, which rather resembled a huge cooking saucepan with a lid. In this receptacle some of Peter's jeans were soaking prior to the - as I mentioned earlier - thankless human task of being washed. At this time Peter was a commercial fisherman (more of that later) and these jeans used to reek of fish when he got home - a wonderful aroma for cats, but obviously not to Sheila; hence the soaking they used to get! Anyway, Coco somehow trod on the lid of this contraption, which immediately turned over and tipped her right into the body of the boiler.

Fortunately the soapy water was cold. Coco was suspended somehow by her front paws, clinging for dear life onto the rim of the boiler. In no way could she manage to scramble out. Her long fur was plastered to her and this made her look like a stick insect with just her cheek fur and fur around her face and head remaining dry and fluffy! How long she was trapped like this they were never sure, but Sheila found her when she returned from work - YES she did work in those days! Anyway, consternation when Coco was discovered and she was hauled out and dried off and given some TLC. Well, she learnt her lesson - be careful where you tread, a rule that as a cat she should automatically have known. Still, we can't all be perfect I know - I am pretty well near it myself but even I have made mistakes at times!

5.00pm   Sheila and Peter arrived home so I went to greet them, relieved that this time they had not brought any of their friends home. I was still sleepy and in a reminiscing mood, so some strangers in the house would have spoiled the quiet atmosphere I needed to reflect and remember times gone by. They made some of that hot brown stuff humans like to drink and sat outside to consume it, surrounded by the Sunday newspapers. I returned to the mat and tuned in the memory again ...

5.45pm   I was thinking about Sasha and Coco and the dog they had to contend with at that time, which was a basset hound called Lady. They must have had an easier time with her, though, than I did coping with a St Bernard and his clumsiness, coupled with his constant drooling over my catsuit! Lady was the owner of a pair of the longest ears that Lucky (who, of course, was the one who told me about all this) had ever seen. When she was taken for a walk around the village, sniffing and snuffling all the time (bassets are habitual vacuum cleaners!), she would sometimes step on her ears and trip up, much to the mirth of passers-by. When she was eating she had to have a special bowl with sloping sides so that her ears didn't drag into her dinner, but even this didn't work all the time and Sheila sometimes had to clip her ears together with a clothes peg above her head to keep them out of the way! One day, Lucky said, Sheila was standing at the cooker and felt something pushing against her and, on looking down, she saw that Lady's pegged-back ears had slipped down in front of her forehead, covering her eyes, so Lady, temporarily blindfolded by her ears, had stumbled into Sheila. Honestly, can you believe that a dog could be so stupid! Well, on reflection, yes I suppose you can! There is just no comparison between a cat and a dog - even the brightest dogs cannot measure up to a cat!

7.30pm   Well, time for my dinner so into the kitchen I went. Beef chunks tonight - not bad, though I've tasted better.

8.00 - 11.00pm Sat on Sheila's knees whilst they stared at the large oblong-shaped silver box in the corner of the lounge. I've said it before - I just do not understand how they are so transfixed by this box. They sit for hours every evening watching it - well, she does. Peter doesn't seem to be able to keep his eyes open for more than twenty minutes or so before he falls asleep, making those revolting - and sometimes quite frightening to a small cat person like me - roaring and whistling noises. How Sheila stands it I don't know, but as she is only half watching the box and also doing various word and number puzzles (using my back as a resting place for her newspaper), perhaps she manages to close her ears to the rumblings echoing over from Peter's direction.

11.15pm Bedtime, and I sank thankfully into my comfy bed and prepared to dream the rest of the night away. Tomorrow would be another day and I would try to recall more memories from the past.

Monday:
6.30am   Well, I could tell it was a weekday (workday for Peter) again, as my wake-up call was at this, such an unearthly and most unacceptable,

hour. Today, though, he seemed not quite so enthusiastic as usual about even his own early start. Something about hating Monday mornings I think he was muttering to himself. He really quite briefly attended to my litter box and then dumped my breakfast dish and refilled water bowl in front of me in quite a brusque manner I thought. Not what I am usually accustomed to - I demand respect at all times from my human carers. Normally I get their deference, but occasionally they do get the odd moody on, and today, I realised, was one of these times with Peter. So, to be on the safe side, I tried to look enthusiastic when he showed me the back door and, in that very slow-motion action that we cats are so good at doing, I did poke my nose outside and finally went out onto the patio. In fact it wasn't a bad day and the sun was already trying to force its rays through the leaves on the surrounding trees - it looked as though later on we would have a nice, warm day. I sat down, surveying things in general, whilst Peter had his breakfast.

9.30am   Peter had been long gone when Sheila eventually swanned downstairs and into the kitchen where I was now sitting in a sunny patch, basking in the warmth of the sun coming through the windows. After our normal affectionate greeting, she gave me a second helping of breakfast and we sat companionably together for a while. Then, after a sigh, she got up, went to the hall cupboard and fetched out a cumbersome machine on wheels with a handle and brushes underneath it, which I absolutely loathe. Dear readers, I have to put paw on heart and admit to you all that I am totally scared of these awful machines - I always have been, ever since I was a kitten. I don't know why - the other cats didn't seem to mind it so very much, but for some reason it has been a lifelong fear of mine. Now I am not one to admit to anything that might detract from my public image of a cool, calm persona of the cat world, but I'm afraid I do hold up my paws to this one phobia.

10.15am Sheila knows of my fear of the procedure she was now going to carry out, so she picked me up and put me upstairs onto my favourite seat in her study where I always feel safe and secure. She then went down and switched on the infernal machine, which made a most dreadful racket - whirring and humming like a huge swarm of angry, outsized wasps. Whilst I was safely away from the machine I did creep out of the study and peeped down through the banisters to see exactly what she was doing with it. She was in the hall below, striding up and down. I've always wondered about why she does this and I still cannot for the life of me think what she sees in it! I thought at one time that perhaps it gives her pleasure - for why else would she do it? - but I don't think it does, because when she comes to put the horrible thing away she nearly always says, "Well thank God that's done for the week!" She walks up and down all the rooms pushing this thing before her - and that's it! When she leaves a room, nothing looks different to me. What a pointless thing to do. I will never understand humans and their whims. Before she usually does this, she has previously gone around the same rooms brandishing a bright yellow piece of cloth and flapping it over and around most of the things in the room. Sometimes, if I am watching closely and the sunlight is shining into the room, I see little clouds of small grey particles rise up, but then, as she passes by, well, they all fall back into the same place again! Another ridiculous and pointless pastime. And she repeats this each week. Why? If it's done one week, surely there's no need to keep on and on doing it. It all beats me. Cats would in no way expend their energy in doing such futile and thankless tasks. What a waste of valuable sleeping or eating time.

11.00am Sheila was now lounging in a garden chair drinking out of a tall mug with steam coming from froth at the top of it, a chocolate biscuit bar named after we cats beside her, and a pile of celebrity magazines, which I know she likes to paw (do you get the pun?) through. I sat nearby, relishing the sun and wondering why Pandy from next door hadn't appeared so far today. Still, I didn't want to tire my mind thinking of him; I was still in reminiscing mode. I was trying to remember more tales of the past that Lucky had told me.

12.30pm We were still in the same places. Sun getting even hotter - it really was a super day and, as Cornwall is often quite a damp place, we were making the most of it. I felt quite hot in my rather heavily furred catsuit, but unfortunately there are no zips in it so I couldn't take it off. Sheila, on the other hand, was sitting in quite a skimpy top and shorts. I wish she wouldn't wear the latter - they don't do her any favours at her age. Still, I do know that she wouldn't wear them in public nowadays, which is probably a relief to the rest of the human race, but with just me around, she doesn't care.

2.00pm Lunch over and the heat still rather hot, I had retired indoors and made myself comfy in the dining room again, and now I am going to tell you a bit more about Sasha the white cat and also Geronimo the blue and gold macaw. Sasha was a real glamour puss, though some people thought the fact that she had one green and one blue eye rather strange. However, I believe that this is quite common in white cats and also they tend to go a bit deaf in old age. Lucky never mentioned if Sasha became hard of hearing or not. That could be used to a cat's advantage I would have thought

- no need ever to come in when you are called on the excuse that you couldn't hear! Anyway, I digress. Sasha was the queen of scallops! When Peter used to be a commercial fisherman, he would bring home all sorts of fishy things. Lucky could even recall a lobster crawling through the hallway one day with the three cats trailing behind it - not that any of them would have actually dared to tackle a brute like that with such heavy and sharp claws. Funnily enough, it is a human conception that all cats love fish; some do, of course, but most would prefer meat. Sasha was the exception to the other cats in the house at that time, i.e. Coco and Lucky. She was the only one that liked fish. Peter used to bring home bags of scallops and would stand at the kitchen sink removing the shells and cleaning them, while Sasha would sit on the draining board beside him and put her paw into the sink, right into the water, which reached up to her armpit, and hook up scallop after scallop. She could eat up to six or seven at a sitting! Friends of Peter and Sheila, who paid quite a lot to eat scallops in those eating places where humans congregate, were always horrified that a cat could also eat posh nosh but for free!

5.00pm   Well, I must have nodded off - all this memory work is tiring! I glanced outside and saw a large magpie on the lawn. That reminded me of when Coco brought one in through the cat flap one day. She was only a few months old at the time and the magpie was as large as she was, if not larger. No way could she have killed the magpie herself, so the humans assumed she had found it recently dead somewhere and just dragged it in. Well, she tried to drag it through, but it got jammed in the opening alongside her. The noise of the flap banging to and fro brought Sheila running and, in due course, Coco and the magpie were freed - Coco to run back to the garden to see if there were any more around, the magpie to the dustbin. Talking of birds made me think of Geronimo, the horrendous macaw! After supper I would recall things about him.

8.00pm   Supper duly eaten and in my comfy spot on Sheila's knee, it was time for me to remember things about Geronimo. Peter, Lucky told me, had always wanted a parrot. He and Sheila had had cockatiels, lovebirds and a cockatoo before (not all at the same time!), but this time Peter wanted a large parrot - well, you couldn't get much larger than Geronimo! Sheila rather fancied a toucan, but in the end, as toucans don't imitate humans' speech, they decided on a blue and gold macaw. In the event, we cats would have much preferred a dumb toucan rather than the loud-mouthed macaw, but we didn't have much choice in the matter! The first thing Geronimo (that was the name given to him in the pet shop) did was to learn the cats' names. He then constantly called in his raucous tones, "Saaaachaaa!" and "Cocooooh" and "Luckeeee", and they were forever running in thinking they had been summoned by the humans! Eventually they learned not to be fooled by the noisy bird! He lived in an enormous cage most of the time, but from time to time the humans took him out with them. When he was safely in the cage, Coco, Sasha and Lucky would venture quite near to see this giant bird (as big as a cat) up close and personal, but if they put their paws up to the bars of the cage Geronimo would give them a sharp nip. Sasha was enormously daring and would spring on top of the cage and let her paw dangle down temptingly just above Geronimo's head. This was her idea of playing the game of chicken - or, in this case, macaw! She was usually quick enough to retract the paw as his evil beak lunged in her direction, but Lucky said that one day he must have caught her because she never played that game of chance again. As I said, Geronimo could imitate human speech and he said all sorts of things apart from calling the cats. Sometimes these things came out at very odd moments and caused hoots of laughter from the humans. At that time Peter and Sheila did not have a motor machine and they used to catch the bus to the gathering place where humans drink those disgusting cans and glasses of coloured liquids, which tend, after due course of time, either to make them giggly and stupid or cross and stroppy. I can never think why humans do this. Pure, fresh water or milk are the best things anyone can drink and they have no ill effects, only good ones. Each to his own I suppose, but there again is a reason why in cat years we live so much longer than humans - we look after our diets and don't consume stuff that harms us or makes us do silly things. Anyway, as I said, they would catch the bus with Geronimo stowed away in a wicker laundry basket, which was large enough to enclose him plus his long tail. One day Sheila was on the bus with the basket, Peter beside her, and the other passengers had no idea there was a macaw inside. Suddenly the familiar raucous tones came up with "What are you doing? Stop it, you old bugger!" The passengers all stared at Peter, thinking he must have been chancing his luck! Peter and Sheila kept straight faces, but the story used to come up quite often when they had friends over. Customers in the communal drinking spots they visited in those days used to love seeing Geronimo and a great fuss was always made of him. People liked to have him sitting on their shoulders and he had a penchant for stealing people's earrings out of their ears, but Lucky used to say that Sheila said he'd never managed to get away with any decent diamonds! Geronimo lived to a ripe old age and was inhabiting part of the conservatory in the next house they lived in - with the large garden - when Tansy and I arrived as kittens to join the family. We were rather in awe of him at first, but we soon became as fed up with him as the rest of the cats did. His continual screeching wore us down (particularly when the signature tune of *Coronation Street* came on), and even when he was asleep he wheezed and snored rather like Peter does now. All in all, we weren't very fond of Geronimo and when eventually, after twenty-five years of living with the humans, he went to a kind of parrot rest home to join many other macaws, we were all delighted and would have thrown our hats into the air if we'd had any! We heard that eventually he died from some sort of respiratory problem in his old age not so very long ago. Certainly his shouting and swearing hadn't affected his longevity!

11.00pm Yawn, yawn - bedtime beckoned. I slipped off Sheila's knee and called into the cat litter igloo en route to my comfy bed. The end of another pleasant day.

Tuesday:
6.40am Here we go again - Peter came into the kitchen awakening me from quite a deep sleep. I must have been dreaming about something good, but for the life of me I couldn't remember what. So I wasn't too cross with him for disturbing me and I was pleased to see that he seemed to be in a better

humour today. I even thought I heard him whistle as he went about the daily litter change and clean-up. The sun wasn't shining, so I had no intention of going into the garden and thought I would wait until he had refreshed the litter before I went on it and performed. This, of course, meant that he had to redo the cleaning job again. I like to keep my eye on him to see that he doesn't shirk this task and gratifyingly he redid it without any complaint. This was now making me a little suspicious - why was he in such a good mood? My breakfast was placed before me and I tucked in, keeping one eye on him. There seemed to be a pile of envelopes on the breakfast bar and whilst he ate his breakfast he was opening them and I realised that it was his birthday. Well, as you who read my diary last year will have known, my birthday came up during the week I was writing. I had a very good time that day, so I hoped Peter would enjoy his day too. He disappeared off to wake up his motor machine and I went through the cat flap into the garden. Pandy was already out there waiting for me. I gave him a quick glance that said both "hello" and "keep your distance", which he understood implicitly. I do have him well trained. So we sat on the patio, savouring the early morning air which, though the sun had not penetrated the clouds yet, was quite nice and refreshing.

9.00am   Sheila appeared in the kitchen and

came out and gave both me and Pandy a few cat crunchy titbits. I like these catty sweeties and Pandy does too. It made us feel quite companionable sitting there together. The sun started to win its battle over the clouds and it really was quite pleasant just sitting and daydreaming the time away. Sheila had disappeared and it sounded like she was using that awful, frightening machine again somewhere in the depths of the house.

11.00am Well, our idyllic time in the garden was rudely interrupted by the arrival of Jason the gardener and his grass-cutting machine, which is even noisier than Sheila's evil machine. Pandy dashed off as fast as he could limp and I quickly went indoors and to my vantage point in the dining room behind the patio doors, where I could feel safe and still make sure that Jason and his sidekick were doing their jobs properly and not missing any blades of grass. Soon the garden looked spick and span again and Sheila was taking the opportunity to have yet another cup of that hot, frothy drink she likes so much, and she had also brought out some more for the gardening lads. They all sat down on the bench and chatted and so I joined them to see what they were talking about. Ah - now I knew why Sheila was looking forward to the rest of the day. Her oldest friend, Lois, was due to arrive and they would all be having a special meal in the evening to celebrate Peter's birthday. Lois comes down to visit each year and we all enjoy her stay here. She generally brings me something nice from a posh store in a place called London, which is somewhere fairly near to where she lives - must be a long way from Cornwall, as it takes her about five hours to drive here in her little motor machine. The machine must look forward to coming here too because Peter always gives it a clean. Lois never seems to do this herself. Peter is for ever cleaning his two motor machines - if Sheila wants to know where he is, she always looks in the motor machines' house first.

1.30pm   Lois just arrived. She looked as well as ever and told me I did too. I thought, cut the cackle Lois - where's my pressie? And, of course, she gave it to me. It was some tins of caviar and tuna cat food for upper-class cats. Well, of course, that's me! I ate half a tin straight off - simply divine! So now off to my mat in the dining room to while away the time whilst the humans sat outside and caught up on all their news. I shall have forty winks and then try and recall some things about Hennessy, that old, slobbery St Bernard dog.

4.00pm   Well the forty winks stretched out into about four thousand winks in the end, but hey, so what! I have all the time in the world to daydream and remember. You, my friends, on the other hand, may not and want to get on, so here is what Lucky told me about Hennessy when he joined the family. As I said in my introduction, he was a really young pup when Sheila and Peter first saw him and fell under his charms; so small, in fact, that they initially told Sheila's father - who was for ever telling them not to have so many pets - that he was only a Jack Russell! Since he grew at a rate of approximately 10lbs per fortnight, they couldn't keep up that pretence for very long! When he was fully grown he weighed over 200lbs - a giant as far as we cats were concerned, but a gentle giant! Sheila had intended to bring Hennessy home in time for her holiday from work in order to look after him full-time, but his breeder wanted her to take him a week earlier. So she took him to her office for that first week, carrying him in a shopping bag! When he was grown up, he could have carried her around in HIS shopping bag! He was from very good stock, so Lucky said, despite not being very astute, and his great-great-grandfather was a Crufts' champion called Bossy Boots. One of his brothers was sold to humans who lived in that alien country across the great pond, and was despatched to them in his own first-class seat on one of those weird machines with wings that hurtle across the sky from time to time scaring me. Yes, I know, I repeat I am an absolute wimp when it comes to facing humans' horrible mechanical and noisy machines. Hennessy's other brother went to be sold in that enormous and expensive store in London that Lois frequents so often. Hennessy had a very soft temperament and he loved us all - humans and cats alike. I'm not sure whether he liked Geronimo though! Did anybody? Lucky, when he was first brought home, went as if by instinct immediately to Hennessy and snuggled up to him, seeing him right away as a huge cuddly, friendly ally. Indeed he was - to all of us - and quite often we used to sleep curled up beside or on top of him at night rather than in our own baskets. He did tend to dribble a lot over our catsuits and to keep cleaning them repeatedly was a pain at times. He was very clumsy and trod on our tails or paws, which also annoyed us, but he was always a soft touch and meant well, so we couldn't say too many bad things about him. I mean, we cats could run rings round him, so anything we wanted him to do, he did. Mind you, any cat can run rings round any dog - it's a fact of life!

7.00pm   I had just finished my dinner, which was pretty unremarkable, as Sheila seemed more concerned about making sure that Lois was fed better than I was! If this happens again I shall take her to task. I expect gourmet food on a regular basis and the humans know this well - it is clearly set out in my directives. On this occasion, though, I will let it lie, as I know that Lois will be giving me bits and pieces from her dinner plate. When she is here, I sit right by her feet so she can't miss me and give her the penetrating "please feed me" stare that always works. She has no pets of her own, so I am something of a novelty to her and she, quite rightly, thinks I am the cat's whiskers, as they say!

8.00pm   The dining room table was covered with multitudinous plates, dishes and drinking vessels (what a wasteful extravagance - one bowl each for food and one bowl for drink is all they really need) and the humans were tucking in to something that looked and smelt like duck to me, though it seemed to be disguised with an orangey, sickly smelling sauce on top of it. I know that Peter has always been very fond of duck, so I guessed this was his birthday treat! Lois duly passed me down several bits of the duck from which, in her thoughtful way, she had scraped off the obnoxious sauce, and they were quite lip-smackingly delicious! Thoughts of my own uninteresting dinner faded away after eating these super morsels!

9.00pm   Sheila, Peter and Lois lounged in their chairs, talking non-stop and only pausing every so often to gulp some strange fizzy liquid out of the huge glasses they were holding, and I was beginning to doze but, before I did so, I recalled a story about Hennessy that became a frequently told story around their dinner table for many months after the event. Sheila was out for a walk with Hennessy one day and they were ambling along a narrow country lane hedged tightly in on both sides with thick bramble bushes loaded with blackberries - a favourite spot with the humans in the autumn when they gathered baskets of these odd things that apparently they loved to eat. Certainly they would never appeal to cats or dogs - didn't smell meaty enough for us. Anyway, in the distance, coming towards them, was a female human in a pale blue coat with a small terrier-type dog. They were accompanied by a male human. The dog was trotting on ahead off the lead and the gap between it and Hennessy was closing by the minute. Sheila always held Hennessy on a tight lead - well, his lead was more of a heavy chain that would have probably hauled up a boat off a beach it was so large! Sheila needed it to hold Hennessy back if he wanted to rush off anywhere! Normally he was slow and placid, but other dogs used to think of him as the humans' cartoon hero, "The Incredible Hulk", because he was so very large, and the majority he met during his walks tended to lunge at him to show they were not afraid of his size! They would often be aggressive to try to show they were unafraid, which I bet they were if one only knew the truth! Hennessy didn't care. He loved any dog - large or small - and always would have liked to have had a run round or game with them, but this never happened because of his size. Shame really, because he was never able to enjoy a good romp with any other dog. Lucky said he used to play with him when he was younger and they had some good games of 'chase', but playing with a cat from your family at home is not the same as playing with doggy pals outdoors! Anyway, I digress again, and meanwhile, the humans plus the terrier were fast approaching. Although the people could quite clearly see that Sheila was holding Hennessy firmly on a short lead and keeping him tight to her side, they made no attempt to call their own dog to them or put him on a lead. If they had done this, everyone would have passed one another without incident and they could have let him off again! So, needless to say, the terrier leapt at Hennessy, and he, in turn, lunged forward towards it. Sheila could not hold on to the lead so she dropped it, and Hennessy - in his usual clumsy way - knocked the terrier head over paws, then knocked the female human in the blue coat right into the hedge and followed this up by immediately also knocking the male human into the opposite hedge! What a commotion! Sheila rushed after Hennessy and quickly grabbed him, checked that the others were all back on their feet again and shouted apologies and they all continued their separate ways, the other two humans literally not saying a word. They must have realised that they should have called their little dog back rather than let it provoke Hennessy, which surely they must have guessed would cause trouble! No sense, some humans! Anyway, the twist in the tail of this little episode was that about three months later Sheila and Peter were at a gathering of humans in their next-door neighbours' house and the couple in the lane were also there! Sheila recognised them immediately and quickly melted away to another part of the room, hoping they would not recognise her!

11.00pm Well, the droning of the humans' voices plus some pleasant background music, coupled with a tummy full of bits of duck, has made me sleep for the past hour or so - I have to keep up my sleep pattern whatever the circumstances. A cat tries to sleep at least 22 hours out of 24 and I generally succeed. Another reason why I am so well preserved for my age - I have never overexerted myself. My batteries are always being freshly recharged during my sleep periods!

11.45pm A rather late night for me but at last the others had all gone upstairs to their own beds. The stuff in the glasses seemed to have made them very giggly. Goodness knows why. As I said earlier, drinking milk or water doesn't make cats giggly! I slid into my bed and looked forward to some more sweet dreams and the prospect of another pleasant day tomorrow.

Wednesday:
6.40am   Peter came rather quietly into the kitchen this morning. He seemed very subdued - strange, I would have thought he would have been buoyed up following his birthday celebrations last night! He seemed to be holding his head and for once didn't try to make me go outside. He also made some groaning noises when he was bending down to see to the dreaded igloo and appeared quite pleased when he realised I had had no need to use it during the night. His breakfast today, I noticed, consisted of a glass of water (much more sensible than that sickly smelling fizzy stuff he was drinking last evening) with a white pill. I wondered if he was giving himself a worming pill? Seems ages since I was last given one by my lovely vet, Mr Kingdon, but I suppose it can only have been about six months ago.

8.00am   Peter had eventually disappeared off to work - I'm never really sure exactly what his 'work' is. He doesn't particularly seem to enjoy it. Certainly it's something that we cats wouldn't consider doing. Why work when you keep servants? Sheila and Lois still hadn't appeared downstairs, so I returned to my bed for a while, which of course is no hardship to me! In that pleasant state of being half asleep and half awake, I recalled something else Lucky told me that had happened with Hennessy when he really had got into big trouble with the humans! Being so large, he had a bed that Peter had had specially made for him, as no basket would have been big enough. Lady the basset hound, on the other hand, had had for years a round wicker basket with which she was very happy. (It doesn't take much to make a simple soul like a basset hound happy). Anyway, when Hennessy was a little puppy he made Lady's basket the object of his attentions when he was teething! He chewed large chunks out of the wicker surround until there was literally nothing of it but a base and a few bits of upright stalks. Sheila saw advertised in one of her magazines a "guaranteed completely indestructible" dog beanbag bed, so she thought this would be just the thing for Lady - a nice, cosy, squashy bed. She duly sent away for it and, one Saturday morning, there was great excitement for Lady when it arrived. It was placed on the floor alongside Hennessy's enormous bed in the cellar room where they both spent their nights, and Lady began the process of examining it and discovering all its comfortable charms. Lucky said that she had told him how excited she was at getting a new bed at last, since Hennessy had ruined her basket. The humans went out for a couple of hours to their local gathering place in the village, thinking what a delightful picture they had left behind them - two happy dogs dozing in their own respective beds. When they returned, however, something of a shock awaited them! The entire room was covered in piles and piles of tiny white beads - so light that every slight draught from the window or the opening of the door sent them flying up and out into every nook and cranny. The "indestructible" bed had several large holes chewed in the cover from which the beads had spewed out! Hennessy was sitting on his bed trying to look invisible, and Lady was mournfully lying by the doorway, wiping her eyes with her ears as she came to terms with the loss of her bed again, without even having had the pleasure of one night's sleep on it! Sheila was furious with Hennessy, needless to say, and the hapless Peter got the task of collecting up all the floating beads, which took him some considerable time, and the air above these beads turned a rather dark shade of blue for some reason that Lucky couldn't quite fathom out! So Lady never did get her super-comfy bed. She managed with another old basket that Sheila had refurbished, as she was not going to waste any more money on something new that Hennessy would ruin. Still, Lady was, as I said, a simple and placid animal, and she never made any great fuss about it. I would have been livid - I take a pride in my possessions. I have two beds, one for the day and one for the night, and I make sure they are regularly cleaned and the covers kept well brushed. Cats will in no way compromise like dogs will. Only the best for us will do!

10.00am I was awakened from my dozing and memories by the sound of the female humans tentatively feeling their way down the stairs. They sat down in the kitchen with hardly a word of greeting for me - very rude I thought - and proceeded to drink some more of the hot stuff they like but this time it was very black in colour and not all frothy as they usually had it. However, they seemed to enjoy it and very soon both of them brightened up a bit and I heard the words "shops" and "shoes" mentioned in the same breath and they disappeared outside and vanished away into the distance in Lois's motor machine.

11.15am I went through the cat flap and settled onto the patio as the sun was now out shining and it was getting nice and warm again. I wondered idly where Pandy could be, but then who should come tippy-toeing by me but the two latest arrivals from next door - Milly and Lily. Sadly, Bob, who I mentioned in my diary last year, is with us no more. A few months after I had finished my diary he was unaccountably knocked over by one of those infernal motor machines and went immediately up to the big cat basket in the sky. His owners were devastated and then, to add to the upset, Ty, who also lived there, decided to move in with some other humans in the area with whom he had formed a great friendship during the daytime whilst the humans in his family were out at their work (tell me, what DO these humans all find so attractive about work?!) So at Christmas two new kittens arrived next door to cheer the humans up. They were the most glamorous kittens I had ever seen - Lily is pale grey-white with very, very long, thick fur and Milly is a few shades darker and more beige in colour. Their tails are to die for - as wide as their bodies! I don't want to sound jealous of their good looks, but I AM! I have always been used to people admiring me and telling me what a nice looking, traditional tabby cat I am, but now, if Milly and Lily are around, all the humans tend to look at them before they realise I am there too. Still, I don't think they are half as talented as I am, so being beautiful is not everything!

11.20am I sat and looked at the two glamour pusses and they sat down nearby and shyly smiled at me. In repose, their facial expression makes them look rather cross, as their Persian breed tends to do, but they do have enchanting little smiles when they want to. They are both still 'feeling their feet' as we say, and as yet have not been too far away from their own home. In spite of being only about six months old, they are really quite mature and I just hope that they, in their youthful innocence, do not come into contact with any of the neighbourhood toms who would be delighted to take advantage of them. Nobody ever took advantage of me, needless to say - nobody ever gets the advantage over Truffles! The girls stayed sitting by me for about half an hour and we made desultory conversation about the weather, the state of the lawns, etc. I asked if they had seen Pandy, but they only knew that he had slept out the previous night and had not been back since. He tends to do this in the summer months, finding comfy places where Jason and his friend have stacked up grass cuttings, or snuggling into the centre of clumps of ferns or soft-leaved bushes. No doubt he would turn up soon!

1.30pm   Speak of the devil - Pandy ambled up. The girls had long gone. I think Pandy is rather nervous in their company - having never had a girlfriend himself, as far as I know, he doesn't really know how to talk to them. With me, the older, attractive but unobtainable female object of his desire, he is far more at his ease.

1.45pm   I was getting a mite hungry - Sheila and Lois were still out, and I had not eaten since breakfast. I examined my bowl again but, however hard I licked at it, nothing was forthcoming. Sheila will be getting a scratch from me if she isn't careful - she has become rather preoccupied with having Lois here and is not paying the attention she should to my wants. This will not do.

2.00pm   I returned to the patio and Pandy, my tail beginning to twitch as I felt a touch of anger coming on about this food business. I lay down with my back to Pandy, as I suddenly did not feel in the mood for light chat. I had intended to do a bit more reminiscing, but that would now come later once I had been fed.

2.30pm   At last - sounds of the humans returning. Sheila and Lois came into the kitchen and dumped a heap of shopping bags on the floor. I stalked in with my ears not up in their usual welcoming manner but lying somewhat flat, so Sheila could tell something was seriously wrong. We do understand each other very well and, despite the language problem sometimes, I can make her know immediately when I am not satisfied with things. I pointedly walked up to my bowl and she started getting flustered and apologising profusely whilst she decanted some nice-smelling stuff into it from another tin that Lois had brought with her. Okay, I thought, I'll forgive you this time for being late with my lunch, but thousands wouldn't! The lunch consisted of a terrine of simply delicious pheasant and venison, so as I gobbled it up greedily I definitely forgave her! She did go outside and gave Pandy - who by that time was slavering over the smell wafting out to him from my dinner - a little taster of it too, so he was also in ecstasies of delight over it!

2.45pm   We all, cats and humans, lay out on the patio companionably side by side - cats dozing, humans chattering. Don't they just go on and on? What on earth do they have to talk about all the time? They never seem to stop and it all sounds so superfluous to me - mostly about hair, those things called shoes that they fix on over their paws, and what the latest human 'celebrities' are getting up to. Boring, boring, boring - still, each to his own I suppose. Cats only make conversation when they have to or there is something important to pass on. As with everything we do, we save our energy and prolong our lives by doing everything in moderation!

4.00pm   I will tell you just a couple more incidents that happened with Hennessy and then that will be the end of the dog talk! In any case, cat talk and reminiscences are far more interesting than dog ones, aren't they? The house that the humans were living in when Hennessy joined them was situated in a small village by the sea, and Sheila used to take Lady and him for walks along the top of the nearby cliffs where there was a large expanse of grass for them to run about off the lead. Not that Lady ever ran very much - Sheila would open the gate at the cliff top and would walk right along the path with Hennessy, sit down for a while perhaps, and then come back again to the gate to find Lady still there snuffling the scents that to her seemed so irresistible! Anyway, on this particular occasion Lady was not with them and Sheila was with her father, who was staying with them at the time, and Hennessy. As the trio meandered along this cliff-top path, suddenly a shout from the beach below made them all jump. It was some humans from the village who recognised Sheila's father and were making themselves known. They were the proud owners of two dachshunds who hated the sight of Hennessy and always rushed at him whenever they met in the village. Hennessy, seeing these two little pests, immediately leapt from Sheila's grasp and started dashing straight down the steep side of the grassy dunes, aiming himself right at the two dogs who, in turn, took to their heels and streaked at full speed right across the beach, heading somewhere in the direction of the village! The humans stood momentarily transfixed as their canine pets vanished from view in a puff of sand, followed by a St Bernard hurtling by. Sheila and her father came panting and gasping down the hill and they, plus the other two humans, followed the direction of the three dogs who were by now completely out of sight. By the time they had reached the village, needless to say there were no dogs to be seen. They walked around asking people if they'd noticed two dachshunds running like mad, pursued by a huge St Bernard - not a sight you would think anyone would miss - but their enquiries came to no avail. Sheila fetched Peter out from their house and he walked around searching for Hennessy for quite a while before suddenly he came upon him being led along by one of his human fishermen friends. Apparently this fellow had seen Hennessy ambling along the street and, as everyone knew Hennessy and who he belonged to, he had grabbed his trailing chain - also managing to cut his hand in the process - with the intention of bringing him back home. He had seen no sign of the other two dogs! (Peter and Sheila heard later that apparently they had fetched up at the back of a car park at the end of the village where their owners had one of those houses on wheels parked. The two dogs sat trembling underneath this contraption until their owners found them, but the good thing about this chase was that they learned their lesson and never taunted Hennessy again). But still Hennessy managed to blot his copy book! Whilst Peter was talking to his pal, Hennessy cocked his leg and filled the other human's rubber boot right up! Honestly, would you credit it? Only an uncouth dog would do that kind of rude thing! Can you imagine a cat doing anything like that? No, no, no! We are so clean in our habits. We do not have to be house-trained like dogs - given a special spot to 'go' on, we USE it and even outside in public we make sure we are tucked away out of sight and always, but always, clean up and fill up our toilet holes. I should have thought that Peter's pal must have wished he'd never bothered to catch Hennessy after that little performance!

6.00pm   My dinner time, and I enjoyed a nice plate of cod and haddock pieces in jelly. I must say that nowadays there are so many different foods around for cats we are spoiled for choice, but, even so, to us the humans' food always seems to smell that much better - as the saying goes, the grass is always greener over the fence - and I myself particularly like the odd stuff they eat called 'cheese'. I am lucky that they realise this and usually I am given a chunk or two if they are eating some. Tonight they all disappeared out and I was left alone to continue my snoozing and remembering.

9.00pm   One more story about Hennessy that I promised you. This time I was around, as it occurred at the big house and garden. It had been a quite normal day and we cats and Hennessy had all been in the garden as usual and the humans were sitting by the pond enjoying the sunset. Suddenly they realised that Hennessy didn't seem to be in sight! They started calling him, but no response. He had never gone missing like that before, so Peter went off one way around the neighbourhood calling, and Sheila the other. However, an hour or so later and they had had no luck. They then decided to go into the communal drinking and meeting place of the local humans to ask there, but on the way they met a friend coming towards them with Hennessy, wearing rather a sheepish look, ambling peacefully beside her! It seemed that Hennessy had somehow got out of the garden and wandered along the road until he came to this place which, because of the nice evening, had its door open in a welcoming manner. Inside, he had gone right up to the bar and had made himself an instant hit with the humans gathered there; hit in more ways than one, perhaps, as - clumsy as ever - he had apparently knocked over several small tables en route and with his ever-wagging, enormous, fluffy tail he'd deftly removed glasses and bottles from the tops of others he'd barged by! But everyone was laughing and nobody seemed to care too much. Various humans had made a great deal of fuss of him and had given him lots of titbits - including cheese (how lucky can you get? Cheese!) and bags of crisps, etc. Because he had no collar on, since at home he didn't always wear it, nobody had known where he had appeared from until Sheila and Peter's friend had arrived. So, luckily again for Hennessy, he was 'rescued' and, from that day on, the humans made certain their gate was shut tight at all times. What a business it must be having to look after a stupid creature like a dog. We cats are far more easy to look after. We don't need constant supervision, or walks, and if we do wander off we are sensible enough to find our own way home again without causing lots of fuss.

11.30pm Loud sounds awoke me from a deep sleep and Peter, Sheila and Lois came back from wherever they had been. I think they had been eating and drinking again - something of a celebratory meal out with the excuse that it was again for Peter's birthday and also because Lois was leaving to go back home again. They came and sat by me and patted me and appeared rather giggly again. I wished they would go upstairs and go to bed and leave me in peace really, but they meant well and thought they were making me happy with their company after leaving me alone all evening. I must say it is nice to feel loved and cared for - you hear of so many ill-treated cats with no comforting human carers - and I know I am blessed with my human family.

12.15am Peace at last - time for bed. Well, I thought it was going to be peace but very soon I was disturbed by the sound of the front doorbell (that awful, loud, clanging sound that makes my fur stand on end!) and the humans' voices somewhat raised. I thought I could also hear some cat cries in the distance, but as nobody came into the kitchen where I was to explain the situation to me, I was kept in the dark - literally! After what seemed an hour but what I suppose was only really about 15 minutes, there was the sound of the front door closing and Peter coming back and going upstairs again. Oh well, I thought, no doubt I will discover what it was all about the following day. I was finding it hard to keep my eyes open, my ears had been straining to no avail, so I slid off into that delightful place I visit every night - slumber land.

Thursday:
6.40am   The morning routine had come round again! Peter woke me as usual and tried his utmost to get me to go out into the garden, but this I had no intention of doing - far too early for civilised cats to get up! Then I left him to it - to tidy last night's litter in the igloo, and prepare my breakfast. I know he kicks at this task sometimes, but it is clearly in his job description and there is just no excuse that I will accept for sub-standard work. I always inspect my toilet area, my water bowl and my adjacent eating area, and he knows that if everything is not up to scratch (yes, I know, another awful pun!) I will be certainly giving HIM a scratch to make the point!

7.00am   The igloo back in its rightful place, clean litter installed and the carpet around it brushed up, Peter put my breakfast down. I sauntered up to it and sniffed. Well, it didn't smell particularly exciting. I'm not even sure what it was - a kind of mishmash of all sorts flavoured with both fish and meat. I then realised it was one of those cheapy cat foods that Sheila tries to slip to me from time to time, thinking she is saving money. I don't like her being deceitful over things like that and I really must take her to task over it. A cat of my superiority should not have to settle for second best at any time, so this miserable breakfast was just not on. Peter was eating his own breakfast. Needless to say, HIS breakfast was one of the top brands of cereal, not like this OWN BRAND stuff he was trying to inflict on me! I rubbed against his ankles to attract his attention and then walked over to the bowl and tipped it right over! Lovely - bits and pieces all over his newly swept floor. I knew that would bring him to his feet! He was muttering specific words about the behaviour of cats both last night and this morning, including an adjective before the word "cats" that began with the letter F, which I really did not wish to know. However, my ploy worked and after he'd cleared up the mess he did slam down my bowl with some different food in it, which I found to be reasonably acceptable. I did not like his attitude towards me, though, so after I had eaten some of the meal, I pointedly returned to my bed, turned my back and tuned into sleep mode again.

8.15am Peter had stamped out, nearly knocking the kitchen door off its hinges going to his work or wherever he was going to that morning, so I decided to go into the garden and see what was happening out there. I went through the cat flap and was greeted by a rather anxious-looking Pandy, who had obviously been waiting for me on the patio. What did he want? I wondered. Well, whatever it was it would have to wait until I had performed my morning ablutions. I strolled towards the nice flower bed at the back of the garden where I have commandeered several sheltered and pleasant spots as my toilet areas. All these are much better on a warm and sunny day than that horrible igloo structure, but, on the other hand, on a cold and wet day the igloo couldn't be more convenient.

8.30am I arrived back on the patio again, having taken my time on the flower bed as I knew Pandy was so agitated and it would show him, once more, my superiority and that if he wants to speak to me or approach me he has to await my pleasure in these things. When you get to my age it is lovely to have a young admirer but, although underneath I am very flattered and also quite fond of him really, I must never let him see it. Pandy then told me what all the commotion had been about the previous night. Apparently one of the girly kittens, Milly I think he said it was, had got out of one of the upstairs windows of their house, tip-pawed along their roof and then - in a somewhat amazing feat - had leapt across a gap of about two metres to get on top of our roof! She was clinging on to the gable end for dear life, for she had almost immediately realised that she would not be able to turn round and get herself back again! So she had started screeching for help at the top of her voice! Her humans eventually heard her and came out to see what had happened. There was Milly, voice getting hoarser and hoarser by the minute, in a very perilous position. Why, I say, do so many cats do this silly thing? They climb up tall trees or fences or leap onto roofs and then get themselves stuck! That is something I have never done - I did naturally get into a good few high places when I was younger, but I always had a plan of action and I looked before I leapt and made sure I could always escape or return to where I had started. That is the essential thing a cat should always do - plan, plan and plan. The humans have an expression "as crafty as a cat" and this is essentially very true - of me, certainly! Anyway, the next-door humans rang our doorbell and Peter came out and saw the situation. Fortunately he had a long ladder and soon Milly was rescued and taken back home very shamefaced. Her humans from that day on made sure their upstairs windows were not opened very wide, but I expect Milly learned her lesson from that escapade and, to my knowledge, she has not been in any trouble since!

9.30am   Sheila and Lois appeared at the back door. Lois was leaving and had come to say her goodbyes. I was sorry to see her go - but she will be down again next year. She patted me and also Pandy, who likes to get pats from everyone he can. I am more circumspect myself - I only allow my humans and their close friends to touch me. I like to know where everyone has been and who they are before I let them put their huge, clumsy paws on me!

9.35am   I followed them indoors and retired to my sunny patch in the dining room behind the patio doors. Time for my morning sleep. Pandy lay down on the patio outside the doors and we drifted off, dreaming our own dreams.

12.30pm My rumbling tummy woke me - Pandy was nowhere to be seen. I strolled into the kitchen and Sheila was already there making herself some nice ham sandwiches. I indicated that I, too, would like some ham and very soon she and I were seated outside on the patio, sun now streaming down on us, agreeably sharing the sandwiches. I must say, it is a cat's life. If one is fortunate enough to have employed the right human carers and they have a comfortable home to share with you, what more can you wish for? It is a pity that so many of we cats (dogs too, of course) are always looking for humans to care for us. When I think right back to the start of my long life, when Tansy and I, as unwanted kittens, were in the animal refuge, it was always packed to capacity. The people who ran it were always desperate for kind humans to take care of the inhabitants, and Tansy and I were lucky that Sheila and Peter took a shine to us and brought us back to share their home. Little did they realise at the time, I suspect, that from then on their whole lives would be taken over by us - but I don't think, in the main, they have ever regretted it.

4.30pm Sheila was lounging on the garden seat, flipping through those magazines about celebrities she enjoys so much - wishes she was one herself I suppose - and I was comfortably ensconced in the centre flower bed with its slate chippings that are so delightfully warm to lie on. Suddenly around the corner came Peter, together with two of their human friends they call Christine and Brian, saying that they were all dying for a cup of that brown stuff they all like to drink. Sheila roused herself and went into the kitchen to get the drinks and the others ranged themselves around on the seats. I looked warily at Christine - she is one of the few people that visit who do not really like cats. Over the years she has mellowed a bit, but the first time she ever came to see Peter and

Sheila in the previous house she was visibly quite scared to find herself surrounded by we five cats! Needless to say, we summed up in one minute that she was uncomfortable in our presence and immediately Tansy and I homed in on her. If a cat sees that a human does not like it, it will always make a point of harassing that human by trying to sit right by them, or even on them, to unnerve them. It always works and is a game that all cats like to play. Eventually, in most cases, the human gets worn down, gives in and pats the cat. Everyone is happy - and it's one up to the cat, of course! Today was so hot that I didn't bother removing myself from the flower bed. The others were all chatting and drinking and eating a Cornish speciality - scones with cream and jam. Ah, cream, I thought, and this did inspire me to get up out of the flower bed and move towards Christine in the hope that she would give me a lick of the cream on her scone! In the event, she didn't - the meanie! Sheila took pity on me, though, seeing I was slavering at the sight of all that cream. She put her plate on the ground and in two ticks I was on to it, licking off all the cream she had left on it. Delicious, gob-smackingly delicious, it was too. Nothing to beat a good dollop of Cornish clotted cream, I say! Then Peter quite spoilt the euphoric moment by saying that 'the cat' (I mean, what did he mean 'the cat' - it's Truffles here, you know, not just 'the cat'!) should not be allowed to eat off her plate! Well, that's a sauce! We cats are amongst the cleanest creatures on the planet - always licking ourselves all over from top to tail and keeping scrupulously clean at all times - and here's him saying in a very discriminatory way that we shouldn't eat off their plates! Well, I certainly wouldn't want him, or any other human for that matter, eating off MY plate, but to say that 'the cat' should not eat off their plates - what a cheek! Well, I was totally affronted! You could say that my front was totally put out! I felt really uptight, so I stalked off and went into my bed and prepared to have a sulk, but Sheila followed me in and calmed me down and said I should not take Peter's comments to heart. It was just a principle kind of thing - he did NOT think I was just 'the cat', but he did have strict rules of hygiene and really she should have remembered that and put the cream into my own bowl. Christine had followed Sheila in and was nodding her head to all this - but then, she wouldn't understand would she? Not being a cat person she probably classes us all as 'unclean' animals like dogs are. Well, it would take me a while to stop bristling over all this and so they both tactfully returned to the garden and I curled up and started to count to a hundred but somehow never reached it - sleep overcame me again! I think I have mentioned before that cats try to sleep at least 22 hours out of 24, and I certainly have always adhered to that custom!

7.30pm   I awoke and saw that the friends had gone and Peter and Sheila were eating their supper in the kitchen. When Peter saw I was awake he did have the decency to apologise for his little outburst and, as the intervening sleep had calmed me down, I graciously accepted his apology and purred at him to say I also apologised for getting a strop on, and had forgiven him completely. I love him dearly, but I know he has some funny ideas - like this example of thinking that humans care more about hygiene than cats - so at times, to keep the peace, we all have to compromise with each other. My dinner was already in the bowl (mine!) and this time it was one of the posh tins that Lois had given me, so I had no complaints there. It was squid rings, Mediterranean style, so eating this gourmet meal quite put me in the best of humour again. I was ready to love everyone and everybody!

8.00 - 11.15pm Sat on Peter's knee for a change this evening whilst they carried on with their usual evening's entertainment of watching the box in the corner of the lounge. I could have done with some earplugs once he started his snoring and wheezing, but mercifully, despite that, I soon dropped off myself, but not before I remembered one more event, that could also perhaps be classed under the category of 'hygiene disasters'. This concerned Hennessy when they were living in the house by the sea, and Lucky, once more, had related this to me. Hennessy was still quite young and sometimes very boisterous, particularly when other humans visited the house and he was greeting them. On this occasion, there had been some kind of problem in the back yard and some men earlier in the day, dressed in trendy, matching overalls, had been doing strange things with long pipes and brushes, all of which they were feeding down into a large square hole outside the back door. Lucky said the hole appeared to be full of a brown-coloured liquidy substance and odd things like pink bits of paper were floating on top of it. Lucky did not know what these things were, but they didn't smell particularly nice to him so he didn't care to examine them too closely. The workmen were sitting down having a meal break when somebody knocked at the front door. Sheila answered the door and in came some friends who, of course, knew Hennessy and patted him and greeted him most affectionately. Hennessy got all excited and bounded back along the passage to the back door, which led down three or four steps. Down he bounced and fell right into the square hole up to his neck! Well, the smell was horrendous! Hennessy scrambled out, covered in thick brown sludge and festooned with bits and pieces of the pink paper hanging off his tail and caught around his ankles. He then galloped around the back yard before one of the workmen, wearing huge rubber gloves, caught hold of him. All the humans were either screaming, shouting or laughing, or doing all of these things at once! Lucky, Sasha and Coco removed themselves upstairs pretty darn quick and Hennessy was hosed down by the humans with lots of water. The whole of the back yard was quite flooded for a while, but it seemed that Hennessy falling into the pit had somehow cleared it of its revolting contents. The workmen's job was done, Hennessy was dried off, the back yard was washed down and swept, the visitors went, and when Peter arrived home from work an hour later he said to Sheila, "Hello dear, had a good day?" He never understood why she threw a towel at his head!

11.25pm Bedtime. Another day over. Sleep beckons once more.

Friday:
6.30am Thank goodness it's Peter's last 'working' day of the week and I won't get woken at this horrible hour tomorrow - two days' respite with two extra hours in bed! Saturdays and Sundays are definitely the best in the week for me. I looked around and through the cat flap and, yes, another nice, sunny day seemed to be dawning. In fact, to my own - let alone Peter's - surprise, I decided to go right into the garden and attend to my ablutions. He was quite amazed, or perhaps

amused, that he didn't have to coerce me into going out so early! I left him to do my housekeeping chores and strolled around the perimeter of the grass. That was still too damp with dew for me to put my paws on. I would wait until the sun had dried it up later. Continuing around the edge, I found a sheltered spot on the flower bed and was soon engrossed in the first performance of the day. I had just finished and was adjusting my catsuit and covering up, when the two young glamour pusses from next door came by. Milly was still a little quiet after her recent excursion onto our roof, but Lily was full of it! She had spotted a rather dashing, black-furred, oriental-looking tomcat peering at her through the back hedge with the biggest pair of golden eyes she had ever seen. She wanted to know if I knew anything about him. Well, I said, yes he certainly has tried to mesmerise me in the past with those huge eyes. But I am past all this lovey-dovey business now, so I had just smiled my Cheshire cat, enigmatic smile and gone on my way. Again, it was nice to know that even at my age I could still attract an eligible male, but, as I've mentioned before, if I had ever decided to get serious, Lucky would have been the only one for me. I indicated to the girls where the oriental charmer lived and they pit-pattered over the damp grass and disappeared in his direction. I returned to the kitchen and my breakfast - food is far more exciting than romance nowadays!

6.50am   I wasn't disappointed - breakfast was shrimps in a light, creamy sauce. It soon disappeared - not even a morsel left for Pandy, who generally receives all my leftovers. Perhaps Sheila could fob him off with the remnants of the own-brand revolting stuff I had rejected the other day! I don't suppose he would care - I don't think he is fussy. Any extra food he can con the gullible humans out of is a bonus to him! Somehow he works it so that he gets two breakfasts, two lunches and two dinners per day - his own plus whatever my humans give him. His acting is definitely worth an Oscar. He has perfected the art of looking dejected and unwanted, starving and lonely. Sheila and Peter fall for it every time. Even today I noticed that Peter had placed a bowl outside the back door for Pandy with what bits I had left from my last night's supper.

8.00am   I inspected the igloo and surrounding area and it seemed Peter had done his job quite well. He had gone off to see his beloved motor machines. I can't see what he sees in noisy, frightening metal monsters like those, but he spends a lot of time with them in their quarters attached to the front of our house, and is always washing and polishing them. He soon disappeared in one of them and peace reigned. I got back into bed for another quick nap before Sheila came down.

9.30am   Down she wandered and on went the noisy little machine in which she makes her hot, frothy drinks. By this time the sun had taken his hat off and was really bright and it was obviously going to be a very hot day - I sighed and wished that on occasions like this I could remove my catsuit. Unfortunately, as I told you earlier, the makers never thought to put any zips in it! Anyway, we went outside and Sheila sat on the seat and I lay under it, grateful for the shade. Pandy very soon joined us and lay down a few patio slabs away, keeping one eye on me, as I was doing on him! The three of us sat quietly and peaceably idling the morning away. I began to recall past events again and I remembered it was a lovely day like this when Robbie joined our group at the previous house. Sheila used to work (you know, I still can't fathom out exactly what this strange thing called work is that nearly all the humans seem to have to do at some time in their lives - it's certainly nothing that cats need to do; we can get along very well without it) in some big building in town and, apparently, one day this very affable and handsome bright ginger-and-white cat appeared seemingly from nowhere and set up camp outside the front entrance. Everyone that passed by patted him and spoke to him and gave him cat treats and bowls of milk, etc. At night the humans would take it in turns to provide him with a dinner - whether it was an 'own brand dinner' I didn't know, but I expect he was grateful for whatever he was given! It was obvious he had come from somewhere fairly close by and perhaps had fallen on bad times. At any rate, he had had the presence of mind to pack his kitty bag and turn up at this place full of humans where he knew he could perhaps obtain help. I have always admired him for that. It takes great courage for a little cat-sized person to think of doing such a thing. At any rate, this all went on for about three weeks, during which time the humans found out that he had originally lived in a nearby road of houses all used by very elderly humans. His own elderly human had passed away to wherever humans go and her relations did not want Robbie and turned him out into the streets - a good example of how some humans are NOT cat lovers! A humans' summer holiday weekend was approaching and everyone was worried about how Robbie would be fed. Nobody could offer him a home, but Sheila, who had originally thought that with having four cats already (me, Tansy, Lucky and Taro) they couldn't take on any more, just could not bear to see him abandoned. She had contacted two cat refuge places, but they had been full up and had advised her to get him 'put down' - another phrase I've never understood; what does it mean? It obviously means something really nasty because she was horrified and immediately made up her mind that he was coming home to join us! Firstly she took him to see Mr Kingdon, the vet, who gave him a clean bill of health, and then she borrowed a basket and arrived back home with him! At the time, her father lived in a little house - rather like Peter's motor machines have now - attached to the main house. Worried about how Robbie would get on with four strange cats, she decided that he would spend the first night with her father to get him accustomed to his new surroundings. I heard from Robbie later that he had been unable to sleep as he was so terrified at the awful wheezing, roaring sounds that Sheila's father made all night! Why is it male humans seem to make this unpleasant and unsociable noise when they sleep? You should be quiet when you sleep. I do not admit to making any annoying sounds, just gentle purring, which is a nice, calming noise - quite hypnotic in its way and I believe humans find a cat's purring to be a real stress reliever. We were all very curious about what was going on in Sheila's father's living area, as we had seen her arrive there with this unknown cat hidden in the basket. It sounded all very suspicious to us and none of us could settle down that evening. However, the next afternoon we were all sitting either in the lounge or the strange oblong-shaped room that adjoined it with transparent walls and roof (a favourite place of we cats to sit in when it was sunny) when Sheila's father let Robbie make his own way through the lounge towards us. When I think of it now, he certainly had some bottle (but then, of course, we knew that from the way he had cleverly gone for help to Sheila's workplace). I don't know what Robbie must have been expecting upon seeing four strange cats of all shapes, sizes and colours, but - using the universal cats' slow-motion walk - he passed right amongst us and lay down under a chair in the transparent room. He then proceeded to ignore us totally, but I bet underneath he was saying, "Phew, glad that's over", to himself! Well, his low-key entrance rather took the wind out of our sails, so we did nothing either! I think the humans had expected fisticuffs and fur flying everywhere! Anyway, from that day on Robbie (well they never knew his real name, but they called him that after Sheila's boss's little pet dog - heaven knows why!) integrated into the family and we all lived happily together from then on.

1.15pm   Time for lunch. Don't the hours just fly by when you are daydreaming or dozing? We, apart from Pandy, went into the kitchen and Sheila threw together some stuff for our meal. She obviously wasn't going to bother making much of a culinary effort today in the heat. I reckoned that she would be getting Peter to fetch in something for their dinner later from the takeaway food place (for humans only, not cats) in the village. I ate a bit of lunch - even I wasn't particularly hungry today - and wandered into the dining room to my favourite place for my afternoon snooze. I had a most delightful scratch - you know, the type when you start off just suppressing a little itch, and then the more you carry on the more enjoyable it gets and you don't want to stop! I can tell you that it was not a flea causing my itch as the humans put drops on my neck every month which, for some inexplicable reason, keep those little devils right away from me. I expect it was a 'heat' itch! Anyway, reluctantly I stopped and fell asleep again.

4.00pm   I woke up and began thinking about Robbie again. After he had been in our company for two or three weeks, the humans decided that it was time to let him out into the large garden that I described earlier. Well, for all his bravado, Robbie became a quivering wreck as he first surveyed the enormous expanse of green grass that surrounded the house! He simply sank down on his haunches, and, if he could have lifted his paws over both his eyes to blot out the terrifying sight, he would have! We couldn't understand it - we all loved the place and thought it was like a huge park full of attractions that any animal would have been happy in. It took about a week before he felt sufficiently confident to start to explore, but after that he became as used to it all as we were. He told me much later that he had spent the entire earlier part of his life in the house of the old lady human and had never been out of doors in all that time. He had spent his days either sitting on her lap or looking out of the window onto a small, dark street with no sign of any green grass. When he had first seen this strange stuff at our house covering everything as far as he could see, he had panicked. Well, I could understand him - when Tansy and I arrived as kittens we, too, had been somewhat amazed at this huge open area and, in fact, Sheila had made us wear infuriating harnesses and took us around initially on leads like dogs wear (we were too young at the time to understand how humiliating that was!) until we got used to it all. In retrospect she was right - we were so tiny that we might have lost our bearings and got hopelessly lost! Robbie was always cheerful, and such a friendly soul with a good word and a smile for everyone, and we all loved him, but he had some very bad luck whilst he lived with us. After about a year or two had gone by he developed something in one of his eyes - a kind of black patch that got larger as time went on and made his eye swell up. It really must have felt extremely uncomfortable, but he never complained. Mr Kingdon, the vet, kept one of his own eyes on it and eventually declared that unfortunately there was nothing for it but to have it removed. Sheila and Peter had an absolute fit at this, but Mr Kingdon assured them that

Robbie would feel happier without it as it was now such an encumbrance to him. Also, he probably hadn't been able to see out of it for some time, he told them, and he could manage quite well with just the other eye, which was perfectly healthy. Nevertheless, the rest of us were very nervous and upset about it all but, typical of Robbie, when the day of his operation loomed he calmly sailed through and made no fuss whatsoever. Mr Kingdon did a very good bit of embroidery, closing up where the eye had been, and was most careful with Robbie's fur, making sure that he still looked handsome but with one eye shut as if he were permanently winking at everybody! It didn't detract from his appearance at all. Even Sheila cheered up as she saw that Robbie himself seemed quite unconcerned about it all. Mr Kingdon had cleverly bandaged one of his front paws up after the operation, so Robbie spent the whole time wondering what had happened to his paw and trying - unsuccessfully - to undo the bandaging! This crafty trick kept his attention from his eye which, in truth, surely must have felt a bit odd. Anyway, all's well that ends well, as they say. Robbie continued enjoying life for several more years before he finally joined the others in their giant cat basket in the sky.

6.50pm   Peter was home and he and Sheila had had a nice-smelling fish and chip supper which, as

I'd surmised, he'd brought in on his way home. They did give me some nice bits of the fish and I also had a reasonable dinner of my own. We were all about to move into the lounge for our nightly sit down when we heard a whirring and banging sound from somewhere above the cooking area where there is a kind of pipe going up through the ceiling. They pricked up their ears - but as their ears are so small you couldn't notice any movement. Mine, on the other hand, were standing right up, as I could quite easily identify those sounds - a bird! How exciting, and inside the house too! Pandy, who was still outside lingering on the patio by the open back door, was also getting quite excited and was hopping up and down on the step, eager to see what was happening. The bird was now fluttering and squeaking - how lovely that sound is to a cat. Many moons now, I'm afraid, since I last caught one. Nowadays I am a birdwatcher not a catcher. Sheila was sure it was actually in the pipe and, although he wasn't sure about it, she finally persuaded Peter to dismantle it. This he managed to do, but no bird! Those words I do not like to hear were being said by both him and Sheila! But still we could all hear it flapping about. My mouth was watering and I expect Pandy's was too. I'm sure we could have winkled the bird out in no time. However, the humans decided to look in the space at the top of the house (somewhere I've never been able to get to and explore as yet) to see if the bird had somehow fallen down from there. Infuriatingly they closed the inner kitchen door so I was unable to follow them. Pandy and I then heard a bit of banging and then the sound of the window in the room above being opened. I went outside just in time to see Peter throw a starling out of the window. It was rather dishevelled and obviously a youngster - prime and tender as Pandy remarked - and it teetered tantalisingly on the edge of the low roof above us. We were both by this time on our hind legs waiting for this unexpected gift from heaven to float down to us, but - just our luck - suddenly it appeared to pull itself together and flew off to another high point on the roof. Well, what a bummer! We well missed out on that one! Oh well, it was obviously not to be. Pandy wandered off disappointed and I went inside again and found Sheila and Peter upstairs looking ruefully at a square hole he had had to cut into the surround of the pipe to extract the unlucky bird. Apparently it had fallen down not directly into the pipe but between that and its protective boxing.

8.15 - 11.00pm Well, we all sat in the lounge and I stretched out on Sheila's knee, thinking miserably of the starling treat I had just missed. She was going on at Peter about him having to make a hole in the wall and he was going on at her about making him unnecessarily dismantle the kitchen chimney - altogether, not a pair of happy bunnies! I put my sleep mode switch in the on position and left them to it!

11.15pm Bedtime.

Saturday:
8.45am   The last day of the week had rolled round again and so I was coming to the end of my diary. Despite not much happening on the home front, the week seemed to have gone by quickly. It had been lovely and warm - perfect weather for we cats - and I had enjoyed looking back and remembering my past feline and canine friends and telling you about them. I hope you have enjoyed hearing about them too! Peter was busy carrying out his cleaning duties around my corner, and I was just about to eat my breakfast before I ventured outside once more.

9.10am   I went out onto the patio and sniffed the air - nice and fresh and, again, it looked as if we were in for a hot day. I performed the usual early morning ritual of carrying out my private functions, followed by fur washing and whisker licking, and strolled back in. Sheila was loading another of her noisy machines with piles of their outer coverings, all types and colours. What a waste of her time! Why can't they be content with the one pale pink outfit they seem to wear underneath? Admittedly, neither she nor Peter look very good in just their underneath skins - perhaps that is why they are obsessed with covering themselves up all the time - but surely SO many different things are quite unnecessary. Likewise, if I go into their sleeping room I see hundreds of those things they, particularly Sheila, fit over their paws and I really can't see why they need to do this. Cats walk, run, climb and go anywhere needing nothing on their paws. Still, as I am continually noticing, humans just do not have the savvy of cats and waste their time and energy on being so disorganised - no wonder they get stressed up and shout out all those naughty words! Cats stay cool, calm and collected, plan their lives carefully and so come out on top every time! Easy-peasy when you know how, and I am a past master at all this, as readers of my last year's diary will already have discovered!

11.30am The humans had gone out and a line of their outer coverings was hanging out in the bright sunlight in the garden. Pandy had not yet made an appearance, so I stretched out on the nice, dry grass and prepared to enjoy the warmth flowing over me. Sleep was flowing over me too - what's new?!

1.30pm I awoke to see Pandy approaching. He has ears as sharp as an owl's and had heard the sound of Peter's motor machine returning. As usual, he dashed round the front of the house to get into the motor machine's home to see if any titbits were forthcoming. (Previous readers will know that Pandy has the perfect food scam. When Peter opens the flap in the side of the house so he can get the motor machine in, Pandy rushes round and hides under the other machine in there and, until Peter bribes him with something to eat, he refuses to budge. This works every time!) Sadly for Pandy, today Peter left his machine outside, so there were no bribes forthcoming!

1.40pm   I went indoors to greet Sheila and Peter and, more importantly, to see if anything had been put out for my lunch. They seemed to be decanting a lot of packages, bottles and cans, etc., onto the kitchen table and I realised they had been doing their big weekly food shop. Yes, thankfully, I could see a stack of tins and packets of my food as well. Good. I noticed that there were no 'own brand' items in the pile today - Peter had obviously taken good notice of my strong hint earlier in the week! Sheila busied herself putting things away and then inserted a couple of items into yet another of her infernal machines. This one to me looks like a smaller version of the big silver box they are glued to each night in the lounge, but somehow quite delicious smells of food emanate from it after a few minutes. Miraculous, and I have to admit that even a clever clogs like me cannot understand just how that particular machine works!

1.50pm   Everyone was now outside in the garden again and the humans were eating some things she'd taken from the machine and said were called 'hot dogs'! How strange - they looked nothing like dogs to me. I've never heard of them - are there 'hot cats' as well? Anyway, they kept dropping me pieces down and I must say they were very tasty. Looked more like sausages than dogs to me! I've always liked a bit of sausage almost as much as a bit of cheese. Pandy winkled out a few bits from Peter too! We all sat happily drinking in the sun for a while - cats and humans in harmony.

3.30pm   The sun by now was really quite hot and I retired under a stone shelter in the garden half asleep again but with one eye on the others. Peter had removed the top of his outer coverings and was exposing his pale pink top half to the sun, but by the end of the afternoon the pale pink had become a browny-pink and his face had turned equally brown but his snout was rather a bright red! Sheila, who did not remove all her top outer covering but did put on those unflattering shorts, was quickly turning a nasty shade of red. Rather unattractive if you ask me - fur comes in much nicer colour schemes. Still, each to his own, as they say! Perhaps they thought being in the sun and turning a few shades darker made them more attractive - exactly to whom I couldn't imagine!

6.00pm   Well, we were all a bit tired after the heat of the day, so Pandy limped off to his own home, hoping for an early dinner there so that he could then come back here and tell his usual 'porkies' to my humans that his own humans never fed him, etc. They always fall for this line, so he knows he's on to a winner and will be given my leftovers as his second dinner. It is always polite to leave a bit on your plate - I rarely clean mine up completely unless I've been eating some of the luxury stuff that Lois brings. Food, food, food - that's all Pandy ever seems to think about! Mind you, he is a bit on the thin side despite all that he crams down. I have always had to watch what I eat as I never wanted to turn out to be a really fat cat. Just to be a nice-sized, cuddly, fat cat was my aim and I've always made sure I've stayed that way.

6.30pm   We all sat outside eating our dinner, although none of us was particularly hungry, it being so hot. Sheila and Peter lolled in their seats and I lay down on the flower bed with the slate chippings that I find so comfy. Once more in a drowsy state, I decided to see if I could remember one last amusing event to put into my diary.

7.15pm   Oh yes, I could remember something that I hope will make you smile. It still makes me do so after all these years! We were all in the garden of the other house and it was a super day like today had been. Tansy and Lucky were sitting at the edge of the pond, peering out to see if there was any movement to indicate that the fish were nearby or maybe any of the other creatures we used to get in there - newts, frogs, dragonflies, water boatmen, etc. Suddenly Lucky spotted a couple of eels approaching. Now, occasionally these strange things - I really don't know if they are fish or animals - did visit. They came from a nearby stream in the next-door field I think. Anyway, we cats had caught an eel from time to time - very difficult I might say. They are so slippery and slimy that even with our sharp claws we've not often been able to hold on to one. Lucky and Tansy jumped up and Taro and myself, hearing Lucky's cry of excitement, also ran towards the pond. The humans never moved, of course, as they did not understand what Lucky was shouting about. The two eels continued on their way towards where we were waiting, two V-shaped ripples on the pond indicating that they were just easily swimming along. Lucky and Tansy were shoulder to shoulder now, ready to pounce as soon as the eels came within reaching distance. We were all in that mixed state of happy anticipation and tension - the lovely moment when you feel that a mouse or bird or, indeed, an eel is about to be caught! But disaster was about to befall us - Hennessy! Out of nowhere he came lumbering towards the pond edge. He had heard the commotion and, never one to sit quietly in the background, was eager to see what was happening. Up he came and in his usual clumsy manner collided with the group of watching cats, knocking Tansy, Lucky and Taro right into the water - NOT me, I'm thankful to say, as I was slightly to one side. Well - splash, splash, splash - in they toppled. The eels immediately took to their heels (I presume eels have heels! Sounds as if they should, doesn't it? Eel heels!) and Sheila and Peter did then dash over to see what was happening. Afterwards they always said they'd wished they'd had one of those little machines they use to take moving pictures handy (another humans' device that I can't get my head around). Lucky immediately swam to the bank, shook himself and climbed back out. Taro followed - very upset and tearful that his beautiful, haute couture, fur catsuit was now all wet and muddy! (He took several days to get over this hiccup to his usual sartorial elegance!) But, worst of all, little Tansy, panicking, paddled wildly and instead of heading towards the bank she went in the opposite direction and ended up on the island! Of course, when she hauled herself up, she realised that she was now marooned in the middle of the pond! Immediately she started caterwauling at the top of her voice, very agitated indeed. We sat stunned, not knowing what to do. Hennessy was trying to apologise to all and sundry (how hopeless was that dog?), but that wasn't going to help Tansy in her situation. So, Peter to the rescue! It was not as easy as it seemed. The pond was not very deep at the edge, about 50cm, but it gradually got deeper towards the middle and the island, where it was well over a metre in depth. The bottom of the pond was thick with sludgy mud and, immediately Peter stepped in, his paws sank right in and he could barely take a step forward. However, he crept on gingerly even though he had soon sunk almost up to the tops of his legs. Sheila was rushing to and fro in her usual helpless kind of way and produced some of those paw coverings they sometimes wear - bright green rubber boots. She, too, got into the water but her boots got firmly embedded in the mud and she stuck fast! Peter was gradually making his way to the island and, some few minutes later, he managed to reach it and pick up Tansy, who was shivering and mewing most piteously. Sheila had to haul herself out of her boots - leaving them embedded in the mud - and scramble back onto the bank herself. I had to hide a smile. Now her legs were all brown, something all her sitting in the sun hadn't achieved! Silly human that she is - why did she get in in the first place? She's never any help in an emergency! Well, eventually everyone was out and dried off. Tansy was petted and comforted and Hennessy was told off once again! Not that any of his tellings-off had ever had any effect but, as I remarked earlier, despite all his clumsiness everyone loved him, so he was never in the dog house for long! All was well in the end and it was a rather funny episode, but it could have turned out to be a disaster if Peter had been unable to reach Tansy.

9.30pm   Indoors we trooped and sat down in the lounge, the humans box-watching again! The week was just about over and my diary complete. On balance, I have had yet another peaceful, happy and healthy year living with my human family and I look forward to the next one and several more too. I probably won't put paw to paper again, though. Two diaries is enough for any cat to write! I do hope you, dear reader, have enjoyed another insight into my life. As you will realise, a cat will never fully understand humans and their strange habits, and humans will certainly never understand we cats and our views on life. However, it is nice to know that, in general, we can all live together harmoniously, isn't it? Give and take and quite often compromise, that's the secret of interactive living! Well, time is getting on and soon bedtime will come round again before yet another day dawns for me!

11.30pm Well, that's it - goodnight and goodbye! Truffles over and out!